HELLO
GF
I HAVE
GREEN FINGERS
SATOSHI
KAWAMOTO

Decorating with Plants

The Art of Using Plants to Transform Your Home

Satoshi Kawamoto

Contents

BROMPTON
KNIGHTSBRIDGE
KENSINGTON ROAD
KENSINGTON GORE
SERPENTINE
KENSINGTON GARDENS
SLOANE ST
164

Introduction

Ever since I got involved in setting up the garden shop Globe Garden in the Mishuku district of Tokyo in 1997, I have been working on developing my own individual approach to gardening. I now feel I am in the process of consolidating a personal lifestyle vision that embraces not only plants but also interior design, as well as the presentation of food. In this book, I have set out to share this vision with my readers. I have used lots of photographs in order to illustrate various design ideas of mine. Please don't feel they have to be reproduced in their entirety. It would be fantastic if there are aspects of these designs that can be adapted to fit your own individual lifestyle. Personally I prefer my rooms not to be over-tidy, so in *Decorating with Plants* I have attempted a comfortable, lived-in look, with nothing arranged in too orderly a fashion. A plant pot here, a book there – it doesn't matter if everything hasn't been put away neatly. I find this makes a room feel more relaxed, and I hope you will feel the same after reading this book.

MANUFACTURE FRANÇAISE
DE
FOURCHES
Action de Cinq Cents Francs
AU PORTEUR

PART

I

Plants in the Home

~ Inside Satoshi Kawamoto's Home ~

Satoshi Kawamoto spent many years renovating his house located on the outskirts of Tokyo. He has transformed what used to be a conventional single-storey residential building into a unique space that overflows with his personality. Here, he shows how his attitude to everyday living has shaped the look of his own home, and shares his ideas, as a top garden stylist, on how to make plants a part of your décor.

THIS is MY HOUSE

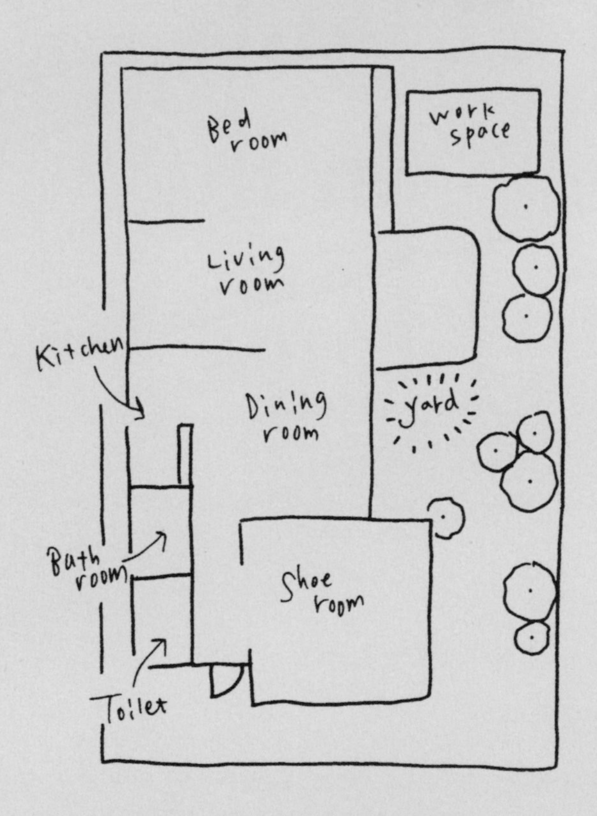
Bed room
work space
Living room
Kitchen
Dining room
yard
Bath room
Shoe room
Toilet

ENTRANCE

Baked by the sun over the years, my welcoming front door is a well-weathered shade of red, which complements the rich blue-grey exterior of the house. I softened the appearance of the concrete garden wall with grooved blocks, and the pale olive-green paint works well with the colours of the front door and the walls. Part of the original garden wall was fitted with a section of railing, which is now concealed behind wooden crates and recycled timber. This helped to soften the formal look. A concrete wall can look dull or even gloomy, but colourful plant pots help to brighten it up.

I used driftwood to create the star above the window.

I've painted the house blue-grey.

The front door opens to reveal a hallway, the walls of which I decorated with leaves taken from old books. A large butterfly specimen is mounted on a page of botanical illustrations. On top of the shoe cabinet I've displayed attractive ornaments, such as antique glass bottles, crystals and dried flowers under glass domes. You can lean a tree branch against the wall and hang a couple of ornaments from it. Alternatively, perch an artificial bird on one of its twigs.

I bought the wall decorations in Paris at Astier de Villatte.

the meaning of S...

making dried flowers.

the wall is decorated with pages from old books – and a real butterfly.

I hung the bunches of flowers next to the mirror to dry in an airy place out of direct sunlight. The process by which plants gradually turn into lovely dried flowers is fascinating to watch. Above the hallway, I created an eye-catching wall decoration using part of an old merry-go-round as a picture frame. The mood of a room can quickly be altered by simply redecorating a frame of this kind. Arrange some dried flowers around it or paste an interesting postcard in the centre.

this picture frame was originally part of a merry-go-round.

WORK
LESS
PLAY MORE
ENJOY
LIFE

SHOE ROOM

This is a room not just for shoes, but also for household tools. You'll find the power drill as well as the shoe brushes in here. It's my private den for the man of the house. Indoor plants with rich green foliage help to create a smart, masculine look. To prevent the décor from becoming too dark, however, I used boldly coloured plant containers in yellow and orange to add splashes of contrast. A feature of this room are the wine crates and vegetable boxes, which, stacked up against the wall, serve as shoe racks. Playing cards were pasted over a disused air-conditioning unit to conceal it.

LIVING ROOM

This is a room for unwinding in, watching some television, perhaps, or a DVD. I use variegated foliage plants in here to introduce more colour and brightness to the room. Try combining dried flowers and pieces of driftwood in among your live plants to create an individual look. The marionette hanging from the ceiling is special to me. I fell in love with it the moment I first set eyes on it. The row of pom-poms along the ceiling works really well with the plants. Don't rely on just one type of accessory to decorate your rooms. Mix, match and combine a lot of different things to create an impact. Go on, be bold!

A Pendleton cushion from the US and a sofa cover made of old military fabric.

A marionette from France.

A friend of my dog 2o

LONDON
AZ
Zzzz.....

Making a special lamp.

I used pale-tinted dried plants, such as eucalyptus, Japanese box and clematis, to create this plant chandelier. For a touch of colour, I combined them with several artificial succulents, chosen to fit in with the colour scheme of the rest of the room. When the light is switched on, fascinating leaf shadows are cast all around the walls.

Yellow tulips make me feel it's springtime.

Floating flowers.

Succulents are easy to care for!

Plants with lush green foliage evoke the refreshing, invigorating sensations of summer, while cheerfully coloured flowers bring the warm glow of springtime indoors. The impression that plants make plays an important role in establishing the mood of a room. Try experimenting with different combinations of plants to ring in the changes. The coffee table in this photograph is an antique wooden packing case with a sheet of glass cut to size and placed on top. Preserved flowers or attractively illustrated greeting cards can be placed beneath the glass to create a personal touch.

KITCHEN

My bright, cheerful kitchen is a delightful place to spend time in, perhaps cooking up a light meal or just brewing some coffee. There is a serving hatch between the kitchen and the dining area: I put different eye-catching collectibles out on the counter according to my mood. The high shelving one finds in kitchens is ideal for showing off the shapely form of trailing plants, which help to add another dimension to the décor of the room. On the wall above the serving hatch, I hung large letters that read 'SOIL'. This is to remind me that earth is everything.

↖ Beans...

Cookie cutters on the mirror frame.

Decorate shelves and ledges close to the sink with fragrant flowers or cuttings from succulents placed in bottles. Something as simple as beads in a glass bottle can make an attractive room decoration. In the evening, light a candle or two to turn the kitchen into somewhere you can relax.

Go ahead and light a candle. they're lovely ...

DINING ROOM

I use this room not only for meals, but also for business meetings. It's the busiest room in the house. Tin panels decorate one of the walls, against which there is a stepladder I converted into shelving to display antique pots, quirky tea cosies, plastic bottle tops discovered at French flea markets and other collectibles that have caught my fancy over the years. A quick and easy plant arrangement can be created by placing pots of plants in a wooden toolbox. High up the wall near the ceiling are antique wall clocks and plates from Astier de Villatte, a collection of which I am slowly building up.

MADE IN THE
NEW YORK
THE
CUIR
MYRRHE
NOTRE DAME
LOS ANGELES 22, CALIF
S
ÉTÉ
FLEURIE

this way to the garden!

this is a treasure of mine, decorated by a designer at Astier just for me.

Dried flowers in an old vase.

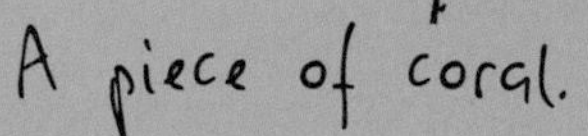

A toolbox can come in handy.

GARDEN

When the room lights are turned on in the evening, there is a fantastical play of shadows cast upon the walls by the plant leaves and the light fittings. I combine soft lighting with candlelight to produce a marvellously atmospheric effect. Because this is the room in which I work on my presentations and design ideas, I have decorated it with plants that are structurally beautiful and have a lot of character – rhipsalis and the staghorn fern (*Platycerium bifurcatum*), for example. A reclaimed antique machine part serves as a plant holder for the rhipsalis.

GENTS

YARD

A garden is not built in a day. Plants possess life force; a garden grows and develops. Dealing with nature's endless cycle of change is a fascinating challenge. My garden has evolved a lot from how I originally conceived it. It's been a process of trial and error. Even after three years I am still at work on it.

↖ My work space

Old keys and religious medallions

I love the colours
of autumn.
Beautiful.

Pots and bricks
Ophiopogon 'Kokuryu'
is a favourite of mine.

To create a relaxing garden you enjoy spending time in, it's important to consider the balance of its component parts. If you take on too much, you won't get any pleasure out of maintaining it, even if your garden is spectacular. Take, for example, the approach leading in to the garden. Attempting to build it all at one go turns the project into a big construction job, and even after all the trouble that entails, the result can still end up looking uniform and characterless. A more individual, settled-in look can be achieved with less hassle if you take time over it, adding new material whenever you have a spare moment or two. Try using different types of materials together. Think of it as completing a gigantic jigsaw puzzle.

'Green' ↓ 'Fingers' ↓

HOMMES

BEDROOM

The bedroom is for resting the body so I keep mine simple. There is a foliage plant with beautiful, bright-green leaves near the head of the bed. But overall, I've avoided overcrowding the room with too many plants. If you use a pot stand in the bedroom, rather than putting the plant pot directly on the floor, the plant is less likely to be damaged by falling objects, and you'll be able to appreciate it from your bed. A calming atmosphere can be created by placing a small lamp next to the plant, so that its light is reflected off the leaves. My antique bedstead is set in the centre of the room, so that as I'm lying in bed I can see all the room decorations, including the swathes of colourful bunting.

BATHROOM

The bathroom is where you get yourself ready to face the world. My bathroom has watery-blue tiles and walls painted in a shade of mocha brown. It's a colour combination I'm really pleased with. I introduced several playful touches: for example, there's a row of tiny ceramic vehicles arranged along the narrow ledge next to the window. Ferns and other damp-loving plants are ideal for the bathroom. Trailing plants in hanging baskets can also look very effective. If there's a window in your bathroom, you'll be able to grow plants. Give it a go!

Wave-polished pieces of glass I picked up on the beach.

Mocha walls and pastel-coloured tiles.

Starfish

Antique keys and bottles

TOILET

The restrained colours of the mirror and picture frames work well against the turquoise-blue walls. The mirror, which occupies a prominent place, has special memories for me, as it was my first serious attempt at producing an antique effect using distressing techniques. The large branches of dried eucalyptus in the corner look spectacular. Eucalyptus is easy to dry and smells wonderful. You can use smaller bunches as hanging displays.

FEATURE 1

Decorating with Plants

Home Renovation

Satoshi Kawamoto on Renovating His House

House

I have been living here for the last three years. It had previously been occupied by a business acquaintance, who thought it would be an ideal property for me to renovate. When he was about to move out, he let me know that it was due to fall vacant. I wasn't able to take up the opportunity straightaway, but when I was ready to move, I was delighted to find the house was still available.

House

It wasn't so much the appearance of the house that appealed to me, but the freedom it offered me to renovate as I pleased. It's not easy to find houses in Japan that one has a free hand to modify. To be honest, I initially thought this house was a bit too old, and I had some tricky moments at the beginning. But now that I've stripped it down and refurbished it, I've become very attached to it. I think I'm very lucky to be living here.

INTERIOR

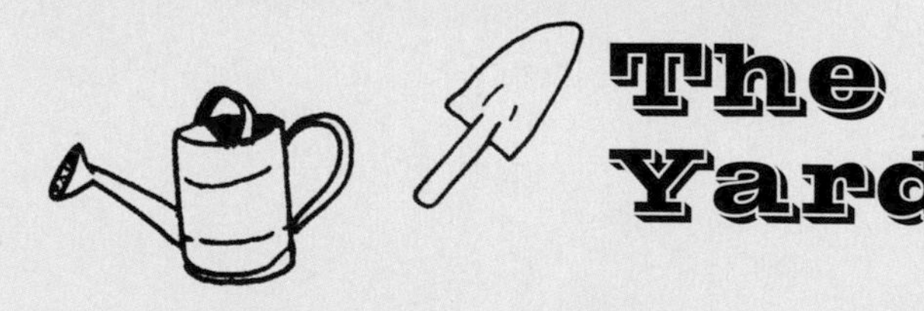

The Yard

The Interior

The house was very traditional in style, and all of the floors were laid with tatami (Japanese woven reed matting), so I had to start by fitting floorboards. I like to use lots of bric-a-brac to decorate my rooms and I thought wooden floorboards would go better with that look. The interior walls originally had a grainy texture in the traditional manner of Japanese houses, and I had to sand them down myself.

The Yard

I am Japanese and I have moments when I am strongly drawn to a Japanese aesthetic. At other times, a stylish fusion of east and west appeals to me more. I often can't make my mind up, but I get a lot of pleasure out of experimenting. When it comes to plants, try out different things. In this way, you will gradually learn what is best suited to the specific conditions of your garden. Take time building up your collection of plants.

The Floor

Painting

The Floor

The matting was covered with sheets of plywood, on top of which the floorboards were nailed. I did the job myself with the help of friends. Antique timber would have been nice but there were cost considerations, so we opted to use new boards, distressed using an oil-based stain and other ageing techniques. To create the feel of an artist's studio, trickle some paint onto the boards or rub in some thinned water-soluble paint.

Painting

I love trying out new combinations of colours. When furniture has been repainted many times, sometimes the undercoat begins to show. I find this effect – created by time and nature – very attractive. I wanted to keep the colour scheme of my house simple, so I chose white for the dining room, beige for the living room and mint green for the bedroom. In the bathroom and toilet, I also used an interesting contrasting colour.

PART

II

Designing with Plants

~ How to Liven Up Your Décor with Greenery ~

This section offers design ideas for those of you who can't decide which plants look best where and with what. These designs don't have to be followed exactly or in their entirety. They're here to help you imagine new ways of bringing plants into your life.

S
STEE

Designing with Stepladders 1

Use a gradation of white, beige and grey tones to create a natural look.

This design concept is perfect for people who love the simple, natural look of linen fabrics and organic cottons. You don't have to use flowers to give your room some flair. Liven it up instead with an assortment of foliage plants with distinctive leaf shapes, colours and habits, including trailing plants and plants with variegated or dentate leaves. Coordinate them with furnishings in shades of white, beige and grey. White candles and bath towels, terracotta pots wrapped with strips of tin plate and dried flowers all work well. If you're worried the effect is becoming too understated, add a touch of vibrancy with something that has a lot of character, such as mint-green tiles or the mirror with the colourful antique tiled frame shown in the photograph below. If a sweet and pretty look is what you're after, try plants with lime-green leaves or white-flecked foliage. Go for dark-green foliage if you want a more mellow effect. You can easily change the impression of your room by using different plants.

Designing with Stepladders 2

Express yourself with unusual plants for a colourful contemporary look.

The approach here is to have fun using lots of colours. Funky, brightly painted plant pots stand out well against more neutral colours, such as whites, beiges and greys. Choose plants with deep-green or bronze leaves for a retro look. Brightly coloured foliage plants look cheery and sweet. You can add a touch of individuality by including succulents or air plants.

Decorating a Corner Space 1

Combine fine foliage with other leaf shapes to create a stylish impression.

Polyscias have bright-green, needle-like leaves and look good together with plants with palely tinted or flecked leaves. The impact of a splendid-looking plant like the polyscia becomes muted if it is used alongside too many plants with similar-looking foliage. Coordinate it with contrastingly shaped leaves for a smart, chic effect.

Decorating a Corner Space 2

Plants with prominent foliage look good composed together with other plants of character.

A large kalanchoe can be very impressive on its own, but it can look more balanced if it's grouped together with other succulents. Because kalanchoes have downy, undulating leaves they also work well together with plants that similarly possess distinctively shaped foliage.

Decorating a Corner Space 3

Show off the shape of your statement plant.

With its twisted branches and trailing leaves, the bottletree, belonging to the *Brachychiton* genus from Australia, makes a spectacular indoor plant. The branches spread out to create the effect of a roomy parasol. Set a chair underneath and gaze up at the fantastic shapes of the branches. Contrasting plants arranged around the base will help to show off its elegant forms.

Decorating a Corner Space 4

Emphasize the vertical by using hanging baskets.

It's easy to make a dull corner interesting by using trailing plants. Hang something like a rhipsalis high up on the wall. Then create a cascade effect by placing more trailing plants on a tall stool. Create a unique container for your hanging plants by decorating it with stickers or your favourite postcards, or by wrapping it in fabric and securing it with hemp string or raffia.

Decorating Walls

1

2

5

6

Use a tool apron as a wall hanging.

Leave some of the pockets empty (1) or pop in a stylish plant in its pot (2). You can use succulents for a masculine look (3). For a retro feel, try bunches of assorted dried flowers (4). Angular plants can look very striking (5), while cut flowers in a small vase look lovely and fresh (6). A fun collectible, such as this mushroom sculpture (7) or this handmade doll (8), adds a casual, playful touch. Just by trying something different you can easily change your room to suit the season or to reflect your mood.

3

MAINE
SUZETTE
LOWE'S
Let's Build Something Together

4

MAINE
SUZETTE
LOWE'S
Let's Build Something Together

7

MAINE
SUZETTE
LOWE'S
Let's Build Something Together

8

HELLO
MAINE
SUZETTE
LOWE'S
Let's Build Something Together

Decorating the Bathroom

1

2

Experiment with different numbers of plants to alter the room's ambience.

Something as simple as using more plants can transform the impression a room makes. The photographs above demonstrate how the introduction of a large pot of ferns can change the feel of this bathroom. Experiment with your favourite plants and change things around to suit your mood. Try a hoya, a dischidia or a syngonium in a pot with its roots showing.

FEATURE 2

Decorating with Plants

WORK CLOTHES

As a plant stylist, I use first-class gardening equipment, but my work clothes are important to me, too. Being stylishly dressed makes me feel good while I'm at work. Like a lot of people, when I see something I like – whether it's brand-named goods or second-hand items – I just have to have it. Looks matter to me just as much as functionality.

SHOP COATS

They don't have to be just for work. They're part of my spring wardrobe. I find mine mainly in second-hand clothes shops. When I see a design that I like, or something tastefully faded or in an unusual colour, I'll often purchase it on the spot.

Each country has its own style of gardening clothes, and I enjoy trying different things out. Second-hand shops are a great resource. Workwear items are comfortable and easy to move around in. They're durable, too. I like how they look, as well as the feel of the fabrics in which they're made, so I don't wear them just for work. You can find things in well-loved name brands. I enjoy learning about the history of various brands, their individual philosophies and their processes of manufacture. It all adds to the interest of the clothes.

Whether it's shop coats, shirts, overalls or footwear, there's so much to choose from these days. They're certainly practical, but you can treat them as items of fashion, too. Getting to know the different types of fabrics, patterns and styles, each with its own history, helps to broaden your horizons. You'll be so much more knowledgeable when it comes to forming your own individual tastes. Using professional gardening clothes and tools can give anybody a real buzz. They look smart, too: even if you don't garden, feature them indoors as room decorations. I can't help thinking my own collection is going to keep growing.

GARDENING BOOTS

My favourite type of boot is lace-ups. Gardening boots are available from different manufacturers in a variety of materials and colours, so choose a pair that suits you and your tastes.

USA

APRON

You don't frequently come across good second-hand aprons, so I make my own in my shop out of old linen fabrics. A stylish work apron works well as a fashion item. Combine it with a matching jacket for going out.

PART
III

Party Settings

~ Using Plants to Create a Warm Welcome ~

When you have people over to your house – whether it's friends, family, work colleagues or that special someone – use greenery to decorate the reception area as well as your tables. Little touches like these help to make the occasion feel special. Set the scene for a wonderful house party by selecting plants that go well with your dinnerware and other furnishings.

ENTRANCE DECORATIONS

Decorate your porch with bunting and other decorations, so that even first-time visitors will be sure to know which house is yours. Balloons, banners and dried flowers in hanging bunches are all good for establishing a festive atmosphere. Choose your decorations to express your personality or coordinate them with the theme of your party.

DESIGN 1

You can stop the look from becoming too saccharine by using bunting made of more masculine materials, such as denim, camouflage fabrics and chino cloth. Combine this with light-coloured plants to create a bright welcome to your house. Prevent the look from becoming too outré by decorating the area around the front gate with some dried flowers.

For a funky look, put up some paper spheres of various colours. Your guests may have to duck in order to reach the front door, but this can be a fun way of creating a sense of occasion. Accessorize with pretty, gaily coloured flowers in pots. Find a way of raising them off the ground so they can be seen.

FRONT DOOR

"reception flowers"

Your guests are going to form their first impression of your home from what they see when the front door opens. What is going to catch their eye first? Something showy? Something calm and soothing? Or perhaps something unique and unexpected? The following pages offer three design suggestions using fresh and dried flowers and accessories.

DESIGN 1

Try wild flowers instead of the usual, brilliantly coloured hothouse kind. Combine their more muted tones with a range of green hues. Succulents and even vegetables can work well with them too. A brightly painted plant pot, like this yellow one, provides some contrast. When you're planning a house party, think about what's going to make your guests feel relaxed. Don't overdo things. Choose items that suit *your* home.

Combine dried flowers, such as baby's breath (gypsophila) and hydrangeas, with dried eucalyptus leaves and dried seed heads. Their mellow colours have a very refined, classical look. Dried flowers and plants are ideal if you don't have the time to deal with the fuss of maintaining cut blooms. You can also add preserved flowers to create an arrangement with more of a contemporary colour scheme.

DESIGN 2

You don't have to use a lot of cut blooms and dried flowers in order to create an impact. Small bouquets tastefully arranged among your everyday things can make your home feel wonderfully welcoming. Make the most of that awkward table top near the front door where you keep your keys and other sundries. Prevent them from looking like clutter by subtly arranging some eye-catching and fun *objets* and knick-knacks among them.

DESIGN 3

try a small bouquet.

After you've dealt with the front entrance, it is time to sort out the dining room. Once the food's ready and you've got everything you need to serve it in, all that's left is to wait for your guests to arrive. When you're designing a party, keep in mind the time of day, the number of guests, the type of food you intend to serve and the style of dinnerware you are going to use.

A HOLIDAY GET-TOGETHER

Is it a public holiday? Why not have some friends around for an informal get-together? The decorative scheme in these photographs was inspired by the time I threw a wonderful impromptu salad together to tide my hungry dinner-party guests over while I was preparing the main meal. The prettily coloured plates work well with the tiled frame of the mirror that I put up on the wall. The dining table has been brightened up with a pale-leaved begonia, which adds flair to the setting without being oppressive.

'Spinach and bean salad'

Antique colours ...

making a flower decoration.

Use old bottles.

The key to this arrangement is to use small glass bottles as flower vases. Cluster them in the centre of your dining table. Be careful not to cram them with too many flowers. Having lots of small vases makes mixing and matching simpler. It will also make it easier for you to reduce the size of your table arrangement as more dishes are brought to the table. You can also take some of the vases along with you when the party moves to a different room after the meal. Try flowers and herbs from your own garden. Even if you have only a balcony, you can still use pots to grow lovely things in.

I complemented the pretty pastel shades of the plates for the salad with refined, neutrally tinted plants. Take special care when using strong colours together. If both your dinnerware and your flowers are in bright, vivid hues, they are likely to clash. Try toning down one or the other.

AN EVENING PARTY

Have a group of people over for good food and conversation at the end of the day. Here, I chose a woodland theme, and I set the table with chunky ceramics and enamelware. The designer pieces are by established, well-loved names. The effect is warm and welcoming, and at the same time it's masculine and earthy. I placed foliage plants with deep-green leaves around the dining table to exude an aura of calm.

'grilled chicken with potatoes and herbs'

Colourful succulents on a tray.

This table display features succulents. They have been taken out of their pots – roots and all – and arranged together on a silver tray. Make the compost a feature of the arrangement, too. Loosen it up for a tastefully informal look. Some succulents have such a striking appearance that they work well by themselves in individual pots. Show their beautiful leaves off to their best advantage. If you're worried your dining table is looking a bit bare, a piece of driftwood is a good thing to use as a centrepiece. It will help to draw all the elements of your table setting together. As a finishing touch, drape the chairs with woollen blankets in mellow, complementary colours.

Decorate the walls with embroidered patches.

I chose various items designed around a wood motif to complement the dinnerware. The spoon and fork with split branch handles aren't practical, but they are fun. Be original and incorporate witty *objets* of this kind in your decorative scheme. If you're going for a warm and mellow effect with your table decorations, liven up your walls for a bit of contrast. Give a white wall a hip look by putting up colourful cloth badges, for example. Don't feel you need to arrange them in neat rows. Spread them out a bit. This way you'll be able to introduce a lot of variety in your decorations, and your eyes will be drawn around the room.

A SUPPER PARTY

This is the kind of intimate meal members of a family, or lovers, might share, when people linger over the dinner table talking to one another in a relaxed, unhurried way, with delicious food bubbling slowly in a pot nearby. Dried flowers and seed heads are a good choice for an occasion such as this. Why not hang bouquets of flowers from the ceiling? You can use lots of pretty and fun things to create atmosphere. This is the style you'll use and adapt most frequently. I accessorized the table with wooden mushroom sculptures and cute candles decorated with bears.

'Ratatouille'

paper flowers
and a stained-glass bird.

Have fun trying out different, subtle combinations of colours. Be playful. The stained-glass hummingbird on the wall looks, from a certain direction, like it's sipping nectar from the hanging paper flowers from Mexico (see page 79). The amazing shape of romanesco broccoli and the incredible colour of red cabbages make them attractive table displays all on their own. I have used white, simply designed tableware and bright-green pot plants to complement the decorations.

A WINE & CHEESE PARTY

It's fun sipping wine with friends under glorious sunshine. But here I went for a chic, retro look that also works well in the evening and under candlelight. Candles are great for creating an intimate setting for a date with your special someone. Make the occasion feel out of the ordinary by serving unusual muscatel raisins in clusters and wonderfully veined cheeses.

many kinds of cheese and dried fruits...

... so well with wine.

Wall decorations can be used as table ornaments!

I brought together some of the wonderful *objets d'art* I've collected over the years to create this look: a bread board made of olivewood, steel flowers created by metalwork artists, sculptures of tree branches from Astier de Villatte in Paris, candleholders decorated with colourful preserved flowers and a bottle made by an artist in LA. What's unifying this look is a retro theme. Picture frames don't have to be used just on walls. Lay one flat on the table and create a charming centrepiece with dried flowers – or with tin soldiers together with delicate little flowers and leaves. For the walls I selected items with elegant clean shapes that look very chic. There are more plates from Astier, as well as picture frames and antique brooches.

FEATURE 3

Decorating with Plants

INSPIRING OBJECTS, INSPIRING PLACES

All homeware and personal accessories sold in my shops, such as Green Fingers, were handpicked and sourced by me. My ability to choose bestsellers depends a lot on honing my tastes overseas. How do I spend my time abroad? How do I respond to new surroundings, and what do I gain from my experiences? Here are photographs taken by me and my friends that suggest some of the sources of my inspiration.

I find going abroad very stimulating because it is all so different from Japan. I'd already been several times to the west coast of the US to source merchandise for my shops. This time around, one of the things I did was to drive up to San Francisco. There were a lot of new discoveries to be made. When I wasn't in business meetings I met up with people or made lists of stores I felt I had to go and visit. Dropping in on bakery stores, barber shops and second-hand clothes shops, I'd frequently come across little touches that would simply blow me away. I try to burn my impressions into my memory as I'm walking around a city.

Each time I'm over here, I make sure to check out the places I know will have the things I like. I go to the big flea markets, such as the ones held in Long Beach and at the Rose Bowl in Pasadena. But I also make a point of visiting places I've never been to before, which I've heard about from friends or read about on the internet. Sometimes I'll meet new people there who will then tell me about other places I have to go and see. As your circle of friends expands, your horizons broaden out, too. I try to be as open-minded as I can and take in new experiences. You don't know what you're going to discover next.

AC.SALICYL.
FOURTH PREMIUM
MISSOURI STATE
CORN SHOW

ROAD
QUES & G
DAILY

What do I gain by going abroad? I usually find lots of exciting things I want to sell in my shops. Then I might suddenly notice that a pair of overalls that a repairman is wearing looks really cool. Or it might be a set of sleek barber's tools laid out on a tray in a barber shop. Or it could be a patch of paint peeling off a wall, creating an incredible effect. The colour of the sky is different in the States and even the air tastes different, but what I really notice are the visual things, like colour and design. I'll suddenly be struck by the décor of an otherwise ordinary-looking store, or I'll get really excited about the way the food has been served in a coffee shop. Those little details are important to me.

PART

IV

Store Designs

~ Ideas for Creating Fashionable Flair in Your Home ~

Here are three very original shops with interiors designed by Satoshi Kawamoto, reflecting his personal philosophy. Merchandise is not merely displayed for sale but incorporated into the shop décor. Satoshi's fresh approach offers new insights into the possibilities of shop design. But there are also plenty of creative tips that can be adapted for the home.

Before

Even before I got to work here, the shop already had a colourful interior, with painted walls and patterned tiles along the shelving. I decided to concentrate primarily on greens for the shop decorations. Eschewing flowers, I created a bright and lively display by using foliage plants with unusual leaf shapes, textures and colours, including variegated and silver-leafed varieties.

OPTRICO

HOLON-R, ground floor
Kita-Aoyama 3-12-12, Minato-ku, Tokyo
TEL 03-6805-0392
www.optrico.com

OPTRICO is run by designer hosiery brand Marcomonde. The theme of the shop is 'Imaginary Lands'. OPTRICO offers selected brand names from abroad as well as Japan. It also sells interior decorations and homeware. The shop interior boasts some fine details: a rug that hangs on the wall behind the till, ethnic-style tiles and the beautiful arches.

I put together succulents and shoe brushes in a silver-tinted box. I playfully placed other plants inside some shoes to make them look as if they are growing there. Have a go at displaying beautiful variegated foliage plants against patterned textiles.

Tall candles surround a plant pot, concealing it from view. A pretty effect is produced by the leaves sprouting between the colourful candles. The subdued colours of the antique teapots and the bust-shaped candles help enhance the vibrant foliage.

Marcomonde socks have been draped around a plant container, creating the effect of a plant-pot cover.

Before

To make the most of the beauty of the wall tiles and their wonderful combination of colours, I was careful not to create a clash with my choice of decorations. A feijoa and a silver elaeagnus amply fill the space in the corner, and the subtly differing colouring of their leaves blends in beautifully with the tiles. I used plenty of plants here, but arranged them in such a way that they do not look overwhelming.

The tin tub fits the colour scheme. It's planted up with just foliage plants, but the effect is showy and elegant.

Unrelated objects can unexpectedly look very good together. Tinware, a straw boater, an old wooden frame and antique medicine bottles are just some of the unusual and varied objects that have been carefully placed here and there against the background of the colourful tiles. The overall effect is well balanced and very smart.

The purplish-pink hue of the tub fits in perfectly with the gradation of colours produced here, from the berries high up the tall silver-leaved elaeagnus, all the way down to the ivies at floor level. Spacing large bunches of similarly hued objects throughout a large arrangement of this kind helps to create a unifying effect.

DogMan-ia

I bring my dog Zorro to this grooming salon for his monthly trim. The distinctive frontage, with its reference to a Dalmatian's spotted coat, has a wonderfully hip look. I complemented it with deep-coloured foliage plants and succulents. Different varieties in a wide range of sizes and with very diverse leaf shapes, combined with furniture and furnishings that have a well-aged feel to them, give a strikingly original, masculine look.

Before

Indoors, there are eye-catching plants with distinctively patterned foliage, as well as chandelier-like hanging baskets, which create a big impact with their size. The globe reflects the fact that there are dog breeds originating from every corner of the world.

Various kinds of succulent are arranged together in an antique pail. A watering can serves as a container for a piece of driftwood. It's all about being creative when combining different plants with unexpected objects. Driftwood and succulents together in an old tin can make a fascinating display. Vary the effect by changing what you put inside your containers according to your own personal tastes and preferences.

THE M.B

biena okubo, ground floor
Uehara 2-43-6, Shibuya-ku, Tokyo
TEL & FAX 03-3466-0138
www.the-mb.net

The style of this boutique is 'French/American'. It offers a unique collection of trad fashions and designer clothes, as well as second-hand and vintage items, from which customers can create their own individual look. To decorate the shop front outside the ladieswear section of the boutique, I use flowers to achieve a feminine look, which, at the same time, avoids being too cloying.

Before

The theme of the cabinet display in the photograph above is 'the gent'. Gentlemen's ties have been hung so that their flowing forms complement the branches of the fabulous trailing plant. The plant pot itself is concealed behind the books on top of the cabinet. The cupboard in the right-hand photograph has been decorated with the image of 'the lady' in mind. I carefully coordinated the colours of the clothing with those of the plants, highlighting the pink tones with touches of black and turquoise.

Ladies

I use frames to draw the eye to the clothes and accessories. Furnishings decorated with star motifs and other interesting pieces such as a chimney pot conceal distracting objects. Trailing plants are wonderful for creating flowing movement in a room. Let the branches hang from high or drape them across a horizontal surface.

FEATURE 4
Decorating with Plants

ARTWORK

My original artwork reflects my vision of life and of the world, but with a distinctive light touch. In these pieces, I find new possibilities for self-expression different from that afforded by my commissioned work.

The Art of Bonsai

ARTWORK

The idea behind the displays captured in these photographs is that they are 'works created in a forest lab nobody has ever been to before'. Bonsai, of course, is now widely known overseas. I wanted to try out my own take on the art form and create hitherto-unseen new worlds in miniature. I like to incorporate preserved and dried flowers, which I think suggest that time has stopped in its tracks, along with pieces of antique machinery that I've been collecting. I am hoping to show more works like these overseas in the future.

Garden Party Lamp

ARTWORK

It's never been easy to find light fittings that look individual, so I have come up with my own concept. I incorporate lace, medallions, feathers, pieces of fabric and pages from old books into my designs to create my unique, somewhat unsettling look. I have hung branches and leaves from the ceiling to create a woodland effect. The tableware is by Astier de Villatte and John Derian. This is a new concept of art: combining plants and art as part of one's total lifestyle.

FORQUE

I have felt for a while that there hasn't been a lot of variety available to people who want a wedding with an original look. To fill this gap, I have created my own brand of wedding accessories, offering uniquely designed personal ornaments as well as table and room decorations, many featuring beautiful dried and preserved flowers.

Product Design

My main work, interior design, is a 3D art form, but I have wanted to express my philosophy in other ways as well, including the merchandise available at my shop Green Fingers. For these products, I have attempted to create original designs that reflect my passion for plants.

Satoshi Kawamoto and Green Fingers

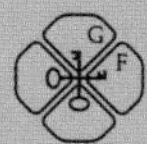

~ All About Green Fingers ~

Satoshi Kawamoto runs four shops in Tokyo, all very different in character but each offering stylish plants as well as decorative homeware and furniture sourced from abroad. Not only are these shops fun to wander through, but also they are places where new discoveries are waiting to be made.

Profile

Satoshi Kawamoto / Green Fingers

As a garden stylist, Satoshi Kawamoto has developed his own distinctive approach, in which he seeks to capture the inherent beauty of plants and the changes wrought upon them by time. He does not, however, restrict himself to plants. He is active in a wide range of areas, managing four shops in the metropolitan Tokyo area, writing for magazines and running workshops. He has designed interiors for major department stores and other retail outlets. Satoshi also runs the designer wedding-accessories brand FORQUE, which offers beautifully crafted personal ornaments and room decorations, using carefully chosen materials such as dried and preserved flowers. Recently he has held exhibitions of his artwork, expressing his response to the beauty of plants. He constantly seeks ways of enriching life by making plants an integral part of one's lifestyle.

Green Fingers

Satoshi's main shop, Green Fingers, is located in the quiet residential district Sangenjaya. It not only offers unusual plants rarely seen for sale, but also stocks a range of antique furniture and furnishings, as well as personal accessories. Entering the shop is like stepping into a secret world crammed with fascinating treasures. The walls are covered with decorative items, and the displays reach up to the ceiling. You will forget the passing of time.

Sangenjaya 1-13-5, ground floor
Setagaya-ku, Tokyo
TEL 03-6450-9541
OPENING TIMES 12:00 – 20:00

GFyard daikanyama

GFyard sets out to offer fresh ideas to people designing their own gardens. The shop deals chiefly with outdoor trees, shrubs and flowering plants. GFyard sells a wide range of unusual and colourful varieties, as well as plant pots, containers and other sundries. You can also view Green Fingers' own show garden here.

Mercury design inc., ground floor
Sarugakucho 14-13, Shibuya-ku, Tokyo
TEL 03-6416-9786
OPENING TIMES 12:00 – 20:00
(varies according to the time of year)

Botanical GF

Botanical GF is located in a large shopping complex in Futako-Tamagawa, a Tokyo suburb. It specializes in indoor plants, and offers a comprehensive selection of varieties – some very unusual – in a choice of sizes. You can also pick a container to match your plant.

Village de Biotop Adam et Ropé
Futakotamagawa-rise SC, 1st floor, Tamagawa 2-21-1
Setagaya-ku, Tokyo
TEL 03-5716-1975 / OPENING TIMES 10:00 – 21:00

KNOCK by GREEN FINGERS

The concept of KNOCK by GREEN FINGERS is to assist customers with suggestions on how to incorporate plants in an interior design scheme. It also stocks a selection of unique plants, many of which have been chosen specifically to suit a more masculine taste.

Next to ACTUS AOYAMA
Kita-Aoyama 2-12-28, ground floor, Minato-ku, Tokyo
TEL 03-5771-3591 / OPENING TIMES 11:00 – 20:00

A
GARDEN
IS NOT
BUILT
IN A DAY

First published in the English language in 2014 by
Jacqui Small LLP
An imprint of Aurum Press
74–77 White Lion Street
London N1 9PF
www.jacquismallpub.com

Original Japanese edition published in 2013 as *Deco Room with Plants* by BNN, Inc.

Author: Satoshi Kawamoto
Photography: Eisuke Komatsubara (Moana Co. Ltd), Satoshi Kawamoto, Eri Tsukimoto (pp. 88–92)
Design: Masanari Nakayama (APRIL FOOL Inc.)
English translation: Yoko Kawaguchi

With assistance from:
ANTISTIC www.antistic.com
STAUB www.staub.jp
H.P.DECO www.hpdeco.com
H.P.DECO Yokohama www.hpdeco.com

ISBN: 978 1 909342 67 5
A catalogue record for this book is available from the British Library.
10 9 8 7 6 5 4 3 2 1
Printed in China

nice plants in your place
GF
TOOLS